little hands
LEAVES

Ruth Thomson

Chrysalis Education

Trees, bushes, and flowers all have leaves.

liquid amber

oak

beech

eucalyptus

dandelion

spotted laurel

horse chestnut

maple

hawthorn

Leaves come in all shapes and sizes.
Some are wide and flat. Others are narrow
and pointed.

The topside of a leaf is tough and smooth.
Why is the tip pointy?
Why is the stalk bendy?

4

topside

The underside of leaves
are usually paler and
sometimes hairy.

underside

Turn a leaf over. Feel the bumpy tubes, called veins.
Food and water travel through them.

Put a piece of paper on top of a leaf.
Rub a soft pencil over it. What can you see?

In the fall, the leaves of many trees change color and fall off.

Collect fallen leaves.
How many colors can you find?

Feel a dead leaf and a leaf growing on a plant.

What do
you notice?

Shuffle through a pile of dead leaves.
What sound do they make?

Some trees have no leaves in winter, but their twigs have buds. Inside the buds are new leaves.

Tree buds are all different.

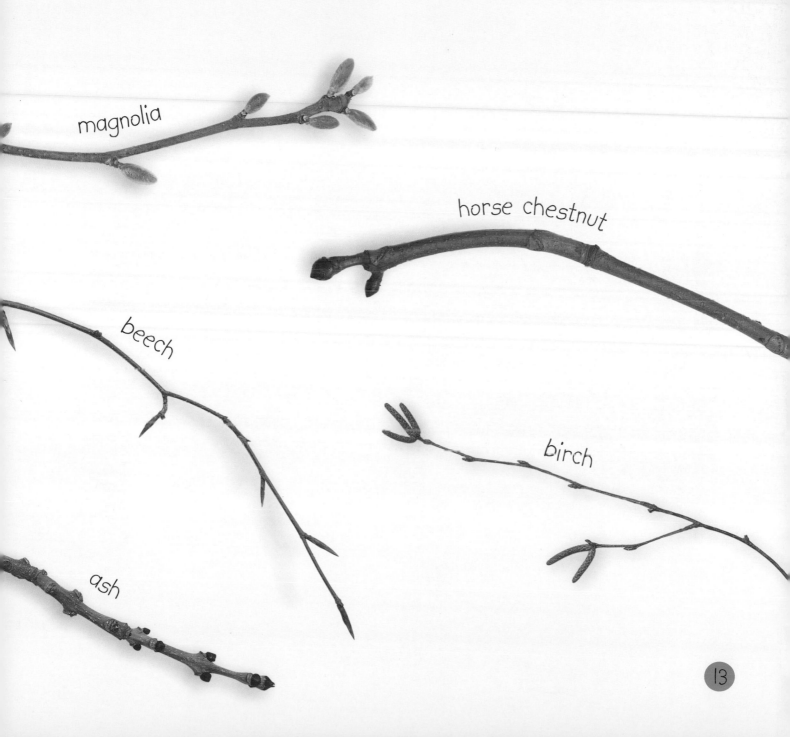

magnolia

horse chestnut

beech

birch

ash

In spring, buds open and leaves unfold.

Flowers unfold from buds as well.

Some plants don't lose leaves in winter. These are called evergreens.

16

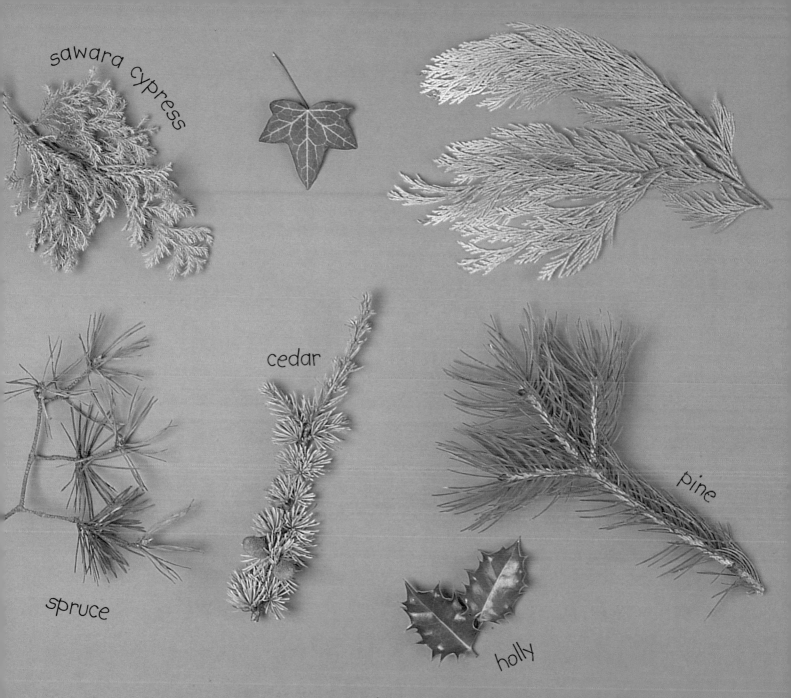

sawara cypress

cedar

spruce

pine

holly

Collect some evergreen leaves.
What do they feel like?

17

Leaves are food for many animals.

Caterpillars eat leaves.

These in the photo eat only nettle leaves.

19

People eat leaves, too.
We eat some raw
and some cooked.

What leaves
have you eaten?

We add scented leaves
called "herbs" to some foods.
Rub some herbs
and smell them.
Which do you like best?

coriander   rosemary   basil   mint

Put leaves between two pieces of paper
with heavy books on top.
Leave them
for a week.

Make a picture
with the pressed
leaves.

Notes for teachers and parents

Pages 2-3

Discussion: Encourage children to see how many different sorts of leaves they can find in a garden, park, or wood. Discuss the differences they notice among leaves.

Activity: Make a collection of leaves. Prompt children to find a suitable word to distinguish the shape of each one. Try long, pointy, jagged, crinkled, fan-shaped, heart-shaped, spiky, or oval.

Pages 4-5

Discussion: Explain that because the topsides of leaves face the sun, they are tough and often glossy to stop the leaf drying out. On a windy day, show children how leaves can bend and sway in the wind, so they don't fall off a tree or shrub.

Activity: Collect examples of leaves with contrasting topsides and undersides for children to feel, so they can notice the differences in their colors and textures.

Pages 6-7

Discussion: Explain that leaves make food and "breathe" for the plant. The leaf stem carries water to the leaf veins and carries food made in the leaves to the rest of the plant.

Activity: Another way to illustrate a leaf's bumpy veins is to make a clay mold of a large-veined leaf. You can make "clay" by kneading 2 cups of flour with 1 cup of salt, 1 cup of water, and 2 tablespoons of cooking oil. Roll the clay out until it is about ¾in thick. Cut it into tiles. Each child can press a leaf, vein side down into a tile so that it leaves an impression. Bake the clay in a low oven for several hours.

Pages 8-11

Discussion: Ask the children if they can work out why some trees lose their leaves in the fall. Suggest that there may not be enough light and warmth for trees to make their food.

Activity: Collect fall leaves and describe their colors e.g. golden, orange, blood-colored, rusty, ginger, muddy, purplish. How about the way they feel e.g. light, dry, crispy, brittle, crunchy.

Pages 12-15

Discussion: Explain that you can identify trees in winter by the color, shape, and position of their buds. Show children how they are positioned on the twig i.e. in opposite pairs or single and alternate. Some are hairy; others are sticky.

Activity: In spring, bring some twigs indoors and put them in a sunny position in a vase of water. Watch the leaves and flowers unfold. (This may take several weeks.)

Pages 16-17

Discussion: Encourage the children to describe conifer leaves e.g. often narrow and needle-like; some sharp and spiky; others with overlapping scales. Notice how they grow, whether singly, in clusters, or bunches. Explain that these leaves can survive the winter because they are narrow and tough, and do not dry out.

Pages 18-19

Discussion: What animals can the children think of that eat leaves (including grass), e.g. cows, sheep, horses, pandas?

Activity: Collect pictures of animals eating leaves and make a collage picture with them.

Pages 20-21

Discussion: Remind the children that eating certain sorts of leaves is good for them as part of a healthy diet. Leafy vegetables are full of vitamins, minerals, and fibre, so they help children to grow, get rid of waste food, and prevent them getting ill.

Activity: Make a list with children of edible leaves. You could make a chart dividing them into those that can be eaten raw, cooked, or both ways. Perhaps you could have a tasting session of different salad leaves.

Index

Distributed in the United States by
Smart Apple Media
2140 Howard Drive West
North Mankato, Minnesota 56003

Library of Congress Control Number: 2004108787

ISBN 1-59389-211-X

Associate publisher: Joyce Bentley
Project manager and editor: Penny Worms

Art director: Sarah Goodwin
Designer: Patricia Hopkins
Picture researchers: Veneta Bullen, Miguel Lamas
Photographer: Ray Moller

The author and publishers would like to thank the following people for their
contributions to this book: Jack Webb, Mollie Worms, Mollie Parker, and
Chris Reynolds of Bedgebury Pinetum in Kent.

Printed in China

10 9 8 7 6 5 4 3 2 1

Picture acknowledgements
All reasonable efforts have been made to ensure the reproduction of content
has been done with the consent of copyright owners. If you are aware of any
unintentional omissions, please contact the publishers directly so that any
necessary corrections may be made for future editions.

Corbis: Patrick Johns 15; Getty Images: Donna Day 11; NHPA Limited: John Shaw
8; Papilio: Dennis Johnson 18, Laura Sivell 19.